T0354639

FANNING THE
FLAME

Igniting Intimacy with God

Kristi M. Young

WESTBOW
PRESS®
A DIVISION OF THOMAS NELSON
& ZONDERVAN

WestBow Press books may be ordered through booksellers or by contacting:

WestBow Press
A Division of Thomas Nelson & Zondervan
1663 Liberty Drive
Bloomington, IN 47403
www.westbowpress.com.au
1 (866) 928-1240

ISBN: 978-1-5127-8866-2 (sc)
ISBN: 978-1-5127-8867-9 (hc)
ISBN: 978-1-5127-8865-5 (e)

Library of Congress Control Number: 2017908152

Print information available on the last page.

WestBow Press rev. date: 05/25/2017

This book is dedicated to believers who are not
willing to settle for a weak or watered-down faith
and who feel a stir to be a warrior for God.

But if I say, "I will not mention his word or speak anymore
in his name," his word is in my heart like a fire, a fire shut up
in my bones. I am weary of holding it in; indeed, I cannot.

—Jeremiah 20:9

CONTENTS

Introduction ix

Chapter 1:   God's Love I

Chapter 2:   Godly Living 23

Chapter 3:   Faith and Trust 49

Chapter 4:   Difficult Times 75

INTRODUCTION

Years ago I began feeling a spark ignite within my soul, a burning that resonated somewhere within me yet did not originate from me. I began to feel challenged with thoughts and questions about faith, about the believer's perspective of God, and about the God of the Bible compared to the God of today. I began to see a huge disparity between the Christian faith and boldness contained within God's Word compared to the majority of the Church today. What changed? Was it the holy and miracle-working God of then? Did His power lessen, His sovereignty wane? The Bible proclaims Him to be the same yesterday, today, and forever. So if He did not change, what or who did?

At least for much of the church in America, the answer is we did; Christians changed. This realization that we have reduced our perspective of God to fit into a man-made box was jarring. Suddenly I realized how our faith has weakened, our boldness has faded, and our absolute submission to—and following after—Him has subsided, largely because we do not truly *know* who our God is.

Christians have become complacent, comfortable, and immersed in the culture around us so that like muscles that atrophy from lack of exercise, our faith has become weak and brittle. Often people question why God does not perform miracles now as He did in biblical times. This line of questioning often leads people to conclude that God is not as powerful now, that He does not answer His children like He used to, and that He no longer speaks or moves or displays Himself like He then. But, I daresay the answer to why we do not see such miracles is not because God has changed or grown distant. It is not because He has become aloof or has given up on our world.

Rather, I believe the answer is because we do not actually expect Him to. If we are truly honest with ourselves (and others), we must admit that while we may at times be bold enough to ask God to move, we do not actually believe He will. Whether it is because we see situations as too large for Him to change, or because we fail to recognize His answers to past prayers and therefore assume that He will not answer now, or, simply, because we do not wait long enough for Him to answer before running after what we want anyway, we very rarely ask in faith.

We have fallen into a pattern of an infantile Christianity, which is primarily driven by our own priorities and life choices, paying lip service to God and occasionally giving Him an hour or two a week to say, "See God: you are important to me." Typically, after all other options have failed, we pray and ask God to help us, but before the last words of our prayers have even left our lips, we pick up the burden and worry again, never giving God the chance to lift it from our shoulders and lead the way.

Impatiently, we accuse Him of failing us, disappointing us, not being loving or faithful or kind, and yet we never *truly* give Him a chance. We refuse to wait and watch for Him to answer our calls for Him to lead, to move mountains, to deliver, and then actually to wait and watch for Him to answer. The issue is not that God is unable to do the impossible, but rather that we have fallen into a place of preemptively concluding that He will not or cannot, because our tiny, pathetic boxes do not have room for believing what we cannot see or understand.

Church, this has to stop. If we are going to declare ourselves to be Christians, to be followers of Jesus Christ, if we are going to claim that we believe in and worship the Lord Almighty, then we must stop reducing Him to only what our limited minds can perceive, and begin seeking Him with every fiber of our being. In the book of Revelation, the letter to the church of Laodicea makes it undeniably clear that God does not want lukewarm followers. He goes so far as to say that He would prefer either hot or cold. Either choose Him or reject Him, but do not sit on the fence. If we are going to choose Him, if we are going to identify ourselves by His name, then it is time for us to be hot for Him. It is time for us to rise up as the army of God and serve Him as our commander and king. It is time for us to offer our very lives to His service and glory.

Each entry of this book includes scripture from God's word. Allow the words to seep into your soul. Allow each verse to challenge your understanding of God and His character, and to penetrate the walls of your self-made God-box. Invite the Holy Spirit to speak to you and draw you deeper into His mystery and wonder. My prayer is that doing so it will awaken a hunger in you for your God. I pray that you will allow the Holy Spirit to fan in you an unquenchable flame of faith. I hope that as you spend time with the Lord and acquaint yourself with who He truly is, you fall head over heels in love with Him, marking the beginning of a deeper journey together beyond anything you could have imagined.

God has not changed. He is truly forever the same, and He wants to display Himself in and through your life in amazing and wonderful ways. Come to Him as a child; give Him a chance to reveal Himself to you. He has so much in store for you!

CHAPTER I

GOD'S LOVE

Consider

Why, my soul, are you downcast? Why so disturbed within me? Put your hope in God, for I will yet praise him, my Savior and my God.
—Psalm 42:5

Praise awaits you, our God, in Zion;
to you our vows will be fulfilled.
You who answer prayer,
to you all people will come.
When we were overwhelmed by sins,
you forgave our transgressions.
Blessed are those you choose
and bring near to live in your courts!
We are filled with the good things of your house,
of your holy temple.
You answer us with awesome and righteous deeds,
God our Savior,
the hope of all the ends of the earth
and of the farthest seas,
who formed the mountains by your power,
having armed yourself with strength,
who stilled the roaring of the seas,
the roaring of their waves,
and the turmoil of the nations.
The whole earth is filled with awe at your wonders;
where morning dawns, where evening fades,
you call forth songs of joy.
—Psalm 65:1–8

Consider this day who God is—this God who, with a word, spoke everything into existence, this God who formed the mountains and carved out the seas and gives every living thing its breath, this God who is infinite in wisdom, strength, and power. Consider Him who steers the hearts of men, who uses every single circumstance to accomplish His divine purpose. Consider this God who holds such majesty and authority that even Satan must answer before Him; this God who calls the sun to rise and to set every day, this God who loves you so much that He sent His Son to this earth to die so that you could live. Consider!

What boxes have you tried to fit God into in your mind? Do you fear His hand is too weak to move an obstacle that stands before you? Do you worry that He is unable to provide for your needs? Are you convinced that a loved one has strayed so far from God that he or she is beyond His reach? Is your hope wavering? Is your trust shaken? Do you question if placing your hope in God is all in vain? Consider this day who God is! Knock down the walls you have constructed that limit your perspective of Him. Take your eyes off your own understanding, your own limited view of this life, and look at Him! There is nothing too large or too difficult for Him and no enemy can stand against Him. You know the end of this story—God wins! Cling to that truth even when it appears all is lost.

When you are tempted to doubt and give way to fear, declare Him sovereign still. When your faith begins to waver, open His Word and allow His Holy Spirit to revive you. He is still the God who formed the earth and all that is in it. He is still the God who answers prayers. He is still the God who forgives our sins and provides salvation. He is still our Rock and our Defender.

Why are you downcast? Why are you discouraged? Consider this day who God is, and remember that the battle belongs to the Lord!

God Loves You

Genesis 1:1–Revelation 22:21

The above might seem like a strange scripture reference. Perhaps you thought it was a typo or that I got confused. But let me explain.

God loves you. He infinitely, unconditionally, immeasurably loves you, not who you could be if you would do a little better, not just who you are on good days or on Sunday mornings when you make it to church. He loves *you*, as you are, right now. He loves all the good, the bad, and the ugly.

All of your strengths and weaknesses during your deepest moments of shame and regret, and when you stand on your highest mountain of resolve and victory—He loves you. He loves you as you read these words, as you accomplish your tasks for the day. He loved you the moment you opened your eyes this morning, and He will love you when you close them to sleep. In fact, He loved you before you even existed.

Before you were born, before He created you, *you* were on His mind. He was thinking of you, smiling because of you, and taking joy and pleasure in you. Before this world was even created, He knew sin and death would separate you from Him. And so He laid out a plan that would cover the cost and grant you salvation to live with Him forever, never to be separated again. It is a plan that would require Him to sacrifice His own Son to die so that you could live.

For many of us, it might be easy to gloss over that, because we have heard it for so long, but take a moment to step back and really consider the cost of what God did. Would you sacrifice your child so that someone else could live? Particularly someone who might or might not even acknowledge what you did? Who might or might not love you in return? It is fair to say that God's sacrifice was beyond our natural capacity or even willingness to love and give of ourselves.

So with this truth in mind and a desire to remind you of God's amazing love, I searched the Bible for the best verses to support that truth. I looked through the Old Testament and through the New Testament, and there was certainly no shortage of scriptures that spoke of His heart. In fact, after trying to figure out how to narrow down the ones to include, I realized none of them are better than any other. God's love is not something tucked away in a handful of verses from the Bible. His love speaks loudly and clearly in every single book on every single page. The entire thing is a letter of love's pursuit, sacrifice, faithfulness, and victory.

Next time you pick up the Bible, regardless of what book you are reading or what chapter you are in, hear His voice whisper to you through every single word. He loves you! He loved you in the past, He loves you in the present, and He will love you for eternity! Amazing grace, amazing love. How truly sweet the sound!

The Source of Light

In the beginning, God created the heavens and the earth.
Now the earth was formless and empty, darkness was
over the surface of the deep, and the Spirit of God was
hovering over the waters. And God said, "Let there be
light," and there was light. God saw that the light was good,
and he separated the light from the darkness. God called
the light "day," and the darkness he called "night."
And there was evening, and there was morning—the first day.
—Genesis 1:1–5

And God said, "Let there be lights in the expanse of the sky
to separate the day from the night, and let them serve as signs
to mark sacred times, and days and years, and let them be
lights in the vault of the sky to give light to the earth. And
it was so. God made two great lights—the greater light to
govern the day and the lesser light to govern the night. He
also made the stars. God set them in the vault of the sky to
give light on the earth, to govern the day and the night, and to
separate light from darkness. And God saw that it was good.
And there was evening, and there was morning—the fourth day.
—Genesis 1:14–19

I did not see a temple in the city, because the Lord God
Almighty and the Lamb are its temple. And the city does
not need the sun or the moon to shine on it, for the glory
of God gives it light, and the Lamb is its lamp. The nations
will walk by its light, and the kings of the earth
will bring their splendor into it.
—Revelation 21:22–24

It is likely that most of us have heard or read the creation story many times through the course of our lives. It is easy to fall into the false thinking that because we have read the Bible and heard the stories many times, we know it all. Recently I picked up my Bible and decided to start reading it again from the very beginning. As I read, I was struck by many things that I had never noticed before, one of which was the creation of light. In Genesis I, we read about the timeline during which God created everything. The very first thing He created after forming the heavens and the earth is light, which in this place means *brightness*. On day one, He says, "Let there be light," and—boom!—there is light. But as you continue to read, you will discover that it was not until the fourth day that He created the sun, moon, and stars. How can that be? If light/brightness existed four days before a source of light was even created, what or who was generating it? Where did it come from?

To answer that question, we must turn to the very last book of the Bible, in which John shares his vision of the New Jerusalem, where we will live with God for eternity. There we discover that place also has light, but the sun and moon are once again not the source. The light there is the glory of God, just as it was at the beginning of creation. And the source—its lamp—is the Lamb, Jesus Christ. In the New Jerusalem, the sun and moon will not be necessary as sources of light because Jesus Himself will live there among His children, and He alone will be the source. But the wonder does not stop there. Not only did God begin as the brightness of light, and not only will He provide all light in eternity, but even now, in this moment, He is our light. The book of 2 Samuel 22:29 says, "You are my lamp, O LORD; the LORD turns my darkness into light."

What seems dark in your life today? What questions are troubling you? What uncertainties are filling your mind with doubts or anxiety? Turn to the Lord with all of it; go to Him now in the midst of all that seems dark and unclear in your life and allow Him to illuminate it. His guidance and wisdom does not depend on anything else in all creation. He does not need to rely on an earthly source to show you the steps to take or give you clarity in this moment. He is all light, all truth. His word is a lamp for your feet and a light for your path. Lean into Him and He alone will shine on you and guide you each step that you take. Even if all else goes dark in the world, He never, ever will. "God is light; in him there is no darkness at all" (I John 1:5).

Be Enlightened

Before reading the below scripture passage, I challenge you to shut out all other distractions. Put down your phone, turn off your television, and take a moment to be quiet. Prepare your heart and mind to hear God speak and let His words soak into you. You may have read the following verses a hundred times before. You may even have them memorized. But right now I challenge you to read them slowly, deliberately, as if you are hearing their message for the first time:

> I pray that the eyes of your heart may be enlightened in order that you may know the hope to which he has called you, the riches of his glorious inheritance in his holy people, and his incomparably great power for us who believe. That power is the same as the mighty strength he exerted when he raised Christ from the dead and seated him at his right hand in the heavenly realms, far above all rule and authority, power and dominion, and every name that is invoked, not only in the present age but also in the one to come.
> —Ephesians 1:18–21

Listen to what God has for you, what He wants to infuse you with, what He stands with open hands ready and wanting to give you if you will just believe Him and accept it. He has called you to *hope*, He has provided a glorious *inheritance*, and He offers you the same *power* that raised Christ from the dead! May God enlighten the eyes of our hearts to begin to grasp and take hold of this God who loves us and provides for us far beyond all that we could ask or imagine!

Unfailing Love

There is no fear in love. But perfect love drives out
fear, because fear has to do with punishment. The
one who fears is not made perfect in love.
—I John 4:18

This is love: not that we loved God, but that he loved us
and sent his Son as an atoning sacrifice for our sins.
—I John 4:10

God is love.
—I John 4:16

Throughout the Bible, there are several references to God's unfailing love. Recently as I was reading through the Psalms, I came upon the phrase *unfailing love*, and it stopped me in my tracks. *Unfailing love* describes a love that will not, cannot, fail, a love that cannot disappoint or abandon, cannot fail or lie or leave the object of its love unprotected. The verse testified to hope stemming from that unfailing love, and it confronted me with the question "Is that where my hope comes from? Do I understand and rest in God's love?"

Often in our journey with God, we pay far too little attention to His heart; we know too little of His love. Our repeated emphasis on trust and obedience, and our focus on surrendering to God's will, while all good and necessary, have caused us to overlook what is fundamentally the most important piece of it all—God's love. In fact, the reason trust, obedience, and self-sacrifice are often difficult, and why we often battle not to give in to fear is because we do not fully understand the love that holds us. The verse of I John 4:18 states that there is no fear in love. This means that in God's love, there is no fear that our trust will be broken, no fear that obeying

God will cause us to be unhappy or miss out in life, no fear that God will abandon, walk away, disappoint, or fail us. God *is* love, and that love is purer and truer and sweeter than any counterfeit version this world could ever offer us.

If we can begin to understand God's love, if we can begin to open ourselves to His love and allow Him to pour His heart into ours, we will find that trusting Him is as natural as breathing and that the notion of not trusting Him is absurd and foolish. We will find that we long to obey and follow Him, because we know that wherever He leads us, His love surrounds us and protects us on every side and will ultimately only lead to our good. We will take joy in offering ourselves to Him because we long to pour out our love to the one who overflows us with His love.

How often does our ignorance to His unfailing love cause God's heart to hurt? How much does His heart break when we cling to fear rather than releasing ourselves into His hands in sweet abandon? I pray that every one of us would allow God to break down the walls we have built around our hearts—walls from past scars, from broken promises, from abandonment. I pray that we would allow God's love to permeate every part of us and heal all the broken and hardened parts of us so that we can rest and live in perfect love. If we allow this of Him, our lives will be transformed. God's love will fill us with the joy, peace, and sweet rest of knowing that in all things at all times, God's love is holding and protecting us and will never let us go.

When all fear is gone and we live in the light of perfect love, the world will see God's love in and through us.

Abba

The Spirit you received does not make you slaves, so that you live in fear again; rather, the Spirit you received brought about your adoption to sonship. And by him we cry, "Abba, Father"
—Romans 8:15

Because you are his sons, God sent the Spirit of his Son into our hearts, the Spirit who calls out, "Abba, Father."
—Galatians 4:6

Shout for joy, you heavens; rejoice, you earth; burst into song, you mountains! For the LORD comforts his people and will have compassion on his afflicted ones.
—Isaiah 49:13

As I was driving to work recently, I heard a song in which there was a lyric that spoke about creation obeying the commands of our Father. I had heard the song many times before, but on this particular occasion that line seemed to stand out louder than all the rest. As I drove, I began to consider its meaning. God has the power, sovereignty, and authority to cause even creation to listen. There is nothing in heaven, hell, or here on earth that can withstand His command. He knows all things, sees all things, and all that exists dwells in the palm of His hand. He can raise an army from dry bones and cause a raging sea to stand still. And yet this God, Who reigns supreme over all, Who has the power to raise up and tear down, this God Who calms the storm with a word, is our *Father*. He is not just our God. He is not just our Redeemer. He is not just our King. He has adopted us as His own sons and daughters and invites us to call Him *Abba*, which in Greek translates to "Daddy." Think of that! He, the Ruler of all things, is your Father!

Consider the intimacy of that title, the compassion and love He offers by adopting us and becoming our Father. Do you realize how much He loves you? How much He rejoices over you? Do you realize that when you hurt, He hurts? When Jesus went to Mary and Martha's house after Lazarus had died, He was speaking with Mary, and in response to her tears and heartache, He wept. He did not weep because of losing Lazarus; He knew in a matter of moments He was going to raise Lazarus back to life. He did not weep out of confusion or despair of the situation; He knew the exact moment Lazarus's last breath left his lungs. He wept because of Mary's tears. He wept because His heart broke over her heart breaking. He knew what was about to come, but in that moment Mary's pain and despair was all she knew, and His heart broke for her.

His love and compassion are just as real and poignant for you as well. He knows that He has unimaginable blessings in store for you, but He also knows that right now, in this moment, the heartache and pain you are experiencing are real. Know that you are not alone in it. He is right there beside you, hurting that you hurt. However, just as with Mary, God knows that if you will just continue to trust Him and lean on Him, even when your heart is breaking, you will see His glory rise out of the ashes. You will see Him truly work all things together for your good, as you love Him and continue on to His glorious purpose.

And so, in the midst of whatever you are struggling with today, despite whatever appears to be dead or hopeless in your life, turn to your Father and lean into Him. Pour your heart out to Him and share your fears, your heartache, your inability to understand why. And once you are done, remember who this Father of yours is. He is the God of the universe; the one who calms the storm and raises the dead to life. There is nothing too hard for Him. There is nothing beyond His ability. Draw your strength from Him, and you will find that even in the midst of the pain, there is comfort and joy.

The Continuity of God

A man came from Baal Shalishah, bringing the man of God twenty
loaves of barley bread baked from the first ripe grain, along with
some heads of new grain. "Give it to the people to eat," Elisha said.
"How can I set this before a hundred men?" his servant asked.
But Elisha answered, "Give it to the people to eat. For this
is what the LORD says: 'They will eat and have some left
over.'" Then he set it before them, and they ate and had
some left over, according to the word of the LORD.
—2 Kings 4:42–44

The consistency of God's character, heart, and ability to do the
impossible can be seen through the Bible from cover to cover. In every
book you will find testament after testament of God displaying His
love for His people, reaching out to save and protect them, and His
ability to provide all that they need through impossible means. One
of the more well-known stories of His provision is the feeding of the
five thousand. Most people learned that New Testament story as
children and know all about Jesus feeding a multitude from just five
small loaves of bread and two fish. What is likely lesser known is
that was not the first time God provided a meal through impossible
means. In 2 Kings, tucked away in three short verses, is a story of God
doing the exact same thing in Israel, long before Jesus did so on the
lakeshore. With just twenty loaves of bread, God fed a hundred men,
with some left over. He saw the need, and as is His way, He provided
more than enough through what appeared to be way too little.

The God of the Old Testament and the God of the New Testament
is the same God today. He can take what is totally insufficient and
lacking and, through it, provide even more than what you need. It is
not difficult for Him. It does not strain against His power or ability.

He speaks, and it is. He breathes and life begins. He gives, and as you put to use what He provides, His supply never diminishes.

What are you in need of today? Strength? Peace? Wisdom? Comfort? Lean into Him, tell Him of your need, and then open your eyes to what He has set before you. He will take what appears to be too little or too small, and with it He will feed the multitudes, leaving you with a remnant that testifies of His goodness and faithfulness to provide.

Remember Your First Love

I know your deeds, your hard work and your perseverance. I
know that you cannot tolerate wicked people, that you have
tested those who claim to be apostles but are not, and have
found them false. You have persevered and have endured
hardships for my name, and have not grown weary.
Yet I hold this against you: You have forsaken the love
you had at first. Consider how far you have fallen!
Repent and do the things you did at first.
—Revelation 2:2–5

Take delight in the LORD, and he will give
you the desires of your heart.
—Psalm 37:4

We all have a unique story of what brought us to the point
of surrendering our lives to the Lord. Mine came after years of
stubbornly trying to do life on my own. It took me hitting rock
bottom to finally look up and call on Him to rescue me. I will never
forget that moment, the moment I called out and asked Him to
take it all. I was instantly overwhelmed by indescribable love—not
condemnation, not crossed arms and a scolding finger, complete,
utter, heart-shattering love. It was as if He said, "*Finally!*" as if He had
been waiting for me the whole time. In that moment, He became my
everything. I wanted nothing more than to spend time with Him, to
get to know Him, and to offer my life to Him for whatever purpose
He chose. He was truly my first love.

Unfortunately, as time goes on and life continues to come at us
with endless demands and we fall into daily routines of to-do lists
and responsibilities, it is so easy to allow that love to dampen. Things,
people, and wants often have a sneaky way of creeping up on to the

throne of our hearts. Before we know it, we are spending our time, efforts, and attention on those matters more than we are on God. He has been knocked down from first place and replaced by idols. Oftentimes, that "thing" that has taken up residence on His throne in our hearts is ourselves. We become our own gods, our own measures of right and wrong, our own declarers of truth. Perhaps we do not abandon God completely. We may still read our Bibles occasionally and do our best to "live as Christians should," but the stark reality is we have forsaken our first love.

Today I invite you to take a trip down memory lane. Think back to that moment when you first experienced grace and forgiveness and unconditional love. Recall that moment when you called on the name of Jesus, and *as soon as you did*, He was there, wrapping His arms around you, declaring you forgiven and free. Fall into His arms again. Delight yourself in Him again—in *Him*, not what He can do for you, but simply in who He is. Kick off the throne everything that has taken His place and declare Him once again the King of your heart, the King of your life, and your first true love.

I Will Never Forsake

I will lead the blind by ways they have not known, along
unfamiliar paths I will guide them; I will turn their darkness
into light before them and make the rough places smooth.
These are the things I will do; I will not forsake them.
—Isaiah 42:16

He who is the Glory of Israel does not lie or change his mind;
for he is not a human being, that he should change his mind.
—I Samuel 15:29

"I will not forsake them." Those are five small, astounding, life-changing, hope-giving, fear-chasing words, spoken by God Himself. It is amazing. How can there still be worry, fear, despair, and doubts? Perhaps it is because so much of life and what we encounter is so uncertain. Practically everything in our lives and the world around us changes constantly: circumstances, settings, economics, relationships, securities. What do we have in life that is an absolute constant? One thing and one thing only—God. He alone is unchanging, unwavering. He does not change His mind. He does not walk away from us. He does not go back on His word. He alone is constant. He alone *is*.

Oh God, break through our tiny minds. Increase our capacity to behold You, to understand You, to grasp the depth of who You are.

Enter His Rest

Come to me, all you who are weary and burdened,
and I will give you rest.
Take my yoke upon you and learn from me, for
I am gentle and humble in heart, and you will find rest
for your souls.
—Matthew 11:28-29

Be still, and know that I am God.
—Psalm 46:10

You, God, are my God,
earnestly I seek you;
I thirst for you,
my whole being longs for you,
in a dry and parched land
where there is no water.
—Psalm 63:1

Do you ever have one of those days when you feel at the complete end of yourself, like if one more challenge, frustration, or obligation comes your way, you are going to unravel? You know the kind. You are tired, worn out, and strung out, and you feel pulled in a million directions all at once. All you want more than anything is to stop, to rest, and to breathe.

This world comes at us like an endless freight train, each car carrying trials and tribulations in an endless variety of forms: pressures at home and at work, bills to be paid, deadlines to be met. And then of course there is the incessant barrage of news stations and social media declaring one crises and tragedy after another without even a pause between each event to allow us to process and mourn the state of our world. We are surrounded on all sides by noise, chaos, and uncertainty. Is this what life was meant to be: a constant race against the clock in a futile attempt to maintain one hundred miles per hour without burning out? Certainly not.

There is a reprieve this side of heaven. It is found when you take a step back out of the race (yes, that is actually possible) and spend time with your heavenly Father. At those times when you feel on the brink of a meltdown, when you feel devoid of peace and calm in the day-to-day, there is a gentle voice calling out to you, a voice inviting you to put it all down, to shut it all off, and to be still. At those times, you will find that what your spirit needs more than anything else is time alone with your Father. Like water in the desert, your spirit depends on Him for rejuvenation.

In those moments when you find yourself desperate for quality time with the Lord, consider this—you miss Him because He misses *you*. You long to have time with Him, because He wants time with *you*. In truth, the only reason you are capable of loving Him is because He first loved *you*. He knows that in and of yourself, you do not have the strength or stamina to get through this life in one (whole, healthy) piece. Without Him, it all loses meaning. He alone is the source of purpose and rest.

Today I challenge you to set aside time to deliberately and whole-heartedly spend time with the Lord. It may be ten minutes, it might be thirty minutes, or it might be an hour. Regardless of how long it is, set that time aside to enter into His presence and just breathe and rest in Him. Push everything else aside—it can wait. What you need more than anything is to be still and know that He is God. Enter into His gift of rest and allow Him to refill you with His peace which surpasses all understanding.

CHAPTER 2

GODLY LIVING

See Them as Jesus Does

A new command I give you: Love one another. As I have
loved you, so you must love one another. By this everyone will
know that you are my disciples, if you love one another.
—John 13:34–35

I pray also for those who will believe in me through their
message, that all of them may be one, Father, just as you are
in me and I am in you. May they also be in us so that the
world may believe that you have sent me. I have given them
the glory that you gave me, that they may be one as we are
one— I in them and you in me—so that they may be brought
to complete unity. Then the world will know that you sent
me and have loved them even as you have loved me.
—John 17:20–23

Recently I was driving home from the airport. It was pretty late in
the evening, and I was anxious to be home. It seems those are the
times when I am most likely to encounter fellow drivers who are not
in as much of a hurry to get where they are going as I am. On this
particular occasion, I found myself behind someone driving below the
speed limit, and I was growing increasingly impatient and frustrated.
As I was anxiously hoping for a passing zone, the thought occurred
to me, I wonder how Jesus would feel in this situation. Would He
get frustrated? I had never truly considered whether or not Jesus got
frustrated or what His reactions had been in everyday situations with
every day people. Once I did, the realization knocked me over and
left me increasingly aware of how far I have yet to go in becoming
like Him.

Typically the reason we get frustrated with people is because
we do not understand why they do what they do (and, even more

specifically, why they do not do what we want them to). That is not the case with Jesus. He knows everything about every person. He knows what shapes and influences our decisions, what fears and anger and scars we are carrying around with us, and what reasons lie behind everything we do or do not do. He knows the depravity of the human condition and how broken each one of us is. He does not get frustrated because He does not expect less than our frailty and brokenness.

But it is even more than that. He does not just know all the whys. It is more than just knowledge and understanding of every person's heart and mind. In the midst of our depravity, He loves us completely. He sees straight into us with overwhelming compassion, pity, and love. He wants to rescue each of us from all the sin and darkness that entangles us and holds us back from the peace, joy, and purpose that He has intended for each one. We are completely known by Him, and His response, His reaction, is *love*. When we make yet another selfish decision or wrong choice, when we respond to situations out of bitter hearts or unforgiveness, He hurts for us and longs to help us out of it, but He never stops loving us.

Imagine if that is how we saw people; not just saw into the why of what they say and do, but if we loved them right where they are in the midst of it. Imagine if we actually followed Jesus's command to love one another with His love. May we never stop pursuing His heart and mind. May we daily lay ourselves and our own perceptions of people down and instead ask Him to give us His eyes, His ears, His heart, His mind. Jesus prayed that we would be one with Him as He is one with the Father. May we never settle for less, whatever the cost. May love be the mark we leave behind as we follow Jesus. That is how the world will know we are His disciples.

Choose This Day

Elijah went before the people and said, "How long will you
waver between two opinions? If the LORD is God, follow him;
but if Baal is God, follow him." But the people said nothing.
—I Kings 18:21

Even while these people were worshiping the
LORD, they were serving their idols.
—2 Kings 17:41

These are the words of the Amen, the faithful and true
witness, the ruler of God's creation. I know your deeds,
that you are neither cold nor hot. I wish you were either
one or the other! So, because you are lukewarm—neither
hot nor cold—I am about to spit you out of my mouth.
—Revelation 3:14–16

Do we understand the concept of undivided devotion? In our culture
where our thoughts and feelings change as rapidly as the weather, do
we know what it is to give something or someone our full allegiance?
I would love to say that, at least as far as Christians are concerned,
we do understand and live with that kind of full conviction, but do
we? How often do we serve God today and reject Him tomorrow?
How often do we waver between two opinions—following the Lord
and following the gods of this world? How often do we serve idols
of greed, bitterness, unforgiveness, pride, and lust, even as we worship
God? How long have we been complacent in living lukewarm lives,
lives that are neither cold toward God nor hot for Him, but rather
tepid and weak?

Time and time again God's word faces us with a decision: either
be for Him or be against Him. Either accept Him as Lord and King,

or reject His offer of salvation and turn away. But instead, we straddle the fence, living with one foot on either side. We are willing to believe that God exists and that He offers us salvation from hell, but at the same time we cling to our own wants and pride.

In Revelation, while addressing the church of Laodicea, Jesus makes it plainly clear that lukewarm living is detestable and intolerable. He challenges us to make a choice: be either hot or cold. Either love Him or hate Him. But stop being lukewarm! Stop trying to live life serving two gods. It cannot be done. Your heart cannot be fully devoted to two things. If you choose God, if you accept His love and salvation through Jesus Christ His Son, and if you declare Him to be King of your life, then stop wavering between two opinions. Stop living for Him on Sundays and for something or someone else the rest of the week. The time has come to choose. God is calling for those who will love Him with *all* of their heart, mind and strength. The time for playing at this Christian thing is over. If you choose God, then give Him everything. Give Him the very breath in your lungs. Offer Him your life, your service, your love, your devotion. Pledge yourself to Him in undivided devotion and leave the rest up to Him.

Choose this day whom you will serve.

Forgive as He Forgave

This, then, is how you should pray:
'Our Father in heaven,
hallowed be your name,
your kingdom come,
your will be done,
on earth as it is in heaven.
Give us today our daily bread.
And forgive us our debts,
as we also have forgiven our debtors.
And lead us not into temptation,
but deliver us from the evil one.'
For if you forgive other people when they sin against you, your
heavenly Father will also forgive you. But if you do not forgive
others their sins, your Father will not forgive your sins.
—Matthew 6:9–15

As far as the east is from the west, so far has he
removed our transgressions from us.
—Psalm 103:12

God demonstrates his own love for us in this: While
we were still sinners, Christ died for us.
—Romans 5:8

Forgiveness. That is a sensitive issue, isn't it? When it is a matter of
receiving forgiveness, we are all avid supporters. The other person
should accept our apology, let bygones be bygones, and that should
be the end of it. How about when it is a matter of being the forgiver?
When someone insults, mistreats, accuses, or lies to you, how quick
are you to forgive them after they have apologized? Or, to take it a

step further, what about when someone wrongs you and never offers an apology? What if they never confess, never recognize their wrong, never take any step to make amends or heal what they broke? How quick are you to forgive then? Maybe it is not even a matter of how quick does it happen, but rather a question of *does* it happen at all?

People are really good at nursing grudges, and Christians are no exception. We allow unforgiveness to take root in our hearts, and the fruit that is produced is bitterness, pride, slander, and an ever-increasing hardness of our hearts. The longer we harbor unforgiveness and cling to the offense, the deeper the roots take hold, poisoning our minds and hearts until it is not just the relationship in question that is affected, but every single relationship in our lives, including our relationship with the Lord. Unforgiveness is a gateway to a plaque that gradually hardens around our hearts that, if left untreated, will rob of us tenderness, love, compassion, an understanding of others, and humility to recognize our own failings and mistakes.

For those who have not received Jesus Christ as their Savior, unforgiveness and the aftereffects should not be all that surprising. They have never experienced the washing away of all sin and having their debt paid for in full. They have not allowed themselves to be redeemed by Christ's blood and experience the amazing freedom from the bondage of guilt and shame that comes along with that.

But what about for those of us who have? What excuse do we as Christians have for withholding forgiveness, for clinging to grudges and offenses, for justifying our doing so because the other has never apologized or recognized their wrong? None! We have completely and utterly no excuse whatsoever. We *have* experienced the washing away of all our sins and having our debt paid. We *have* been redeemed by Christ's blood, and daily we live in the freedom that He has offered us through His sacrifice. And did we apologize to Jesus before He forgave us? Did we recognize our own guilt and wrongdoing prior to His choosing to be crucified on the cross so that we did not have to rightfully die? No. While we were still sinners, while we were still continuing on in our sin, Christ died for us. He did not choose to forgive us in response to an eloquent apology. He chose to forgive us even as we continued to reject Him, falsely accuse Him, and insist we wanted nothing to do with Him. He chose to forgive because He chose to love.

Today, take a few moments to examine your hearts, minds, and attitudes. Are you harboring unforgiveness? Have you grown bitter and hard and resentful? Stop being so quick to defend yourself by saying, "Yeah, but you do not know what so and so did; how they hurt me." Your pain is real, that is not denied, but the truth is no one has ever done to us what we did to Christ. No one has ever hurt us as deeply as we hurt Him. And yet He forgives. So if you have accepted His forgiveness, which He offered long before you ever acknowledged any remorse, you must too offer that same forgiveness. He will help you do so. He will give you the strength and healing you need to take that step. But you need to release your grip on the offense and allow Him to remove all the roots that have settled down inside. Remember His amazing grace and forgive as He has forgiven you.

In Those Days

In those days Israel had no king; everyone did as they saw fit.
—Judges 17:6

Four times throughout the book of Judges, the author states "in those days Israel had no king." That book was written before kings were established in the nation of Israel, so it must refer to more than simply not having an earthly king. If you read through the stories contained in that book, you will quickly discover what that truly meant—even God was not their King. The Israelites turned away from following and seeking Him, and the effect was catastrophic and gruesome: wars among the tribes, idolatry, violence, rape, and kidnapping. The nation fell into a time when they answered to no one but their own selfish, sinful motivations, and the results are heartbreaking.

It is easy to liken that to the state of our own nation and see the undeniable effects of our turning away from God. Our society is driven by one thing –me. We have become the be-all and end-all of what is right for us, and no one ought to dare try to tell us we are wrong. We have turned away from God, and the result is perversion, loss of absolute truth, and chaos and violence at every turn.

But let us drill it down even more than that. Israel was God's chosen people. Likewise, as Christians we are His people. So how do we compare to the people of God at that time? Our initial instinct is probably to defend ourselves and say we have not turned away from God *that* much; we are not as violent or disobedient as they were. But let us take an honest look before we pat ourselves on the back.

We may not go to war against our fellow Christians physically, but how many battles happen between churches and denominations? We may not murder each other, but how much hate brews beneath the surface, how much unforgiveness? We may not build shrines to other gods in our homes, but how many of us have made idols of our possessions, our jobs, our families, or ourselves? How many of us allow ourselves to be riddled with fear, anxiety and doubt because we choose to focus on what we see around us rather than trusting and resting in our King to protect and lead us? It is a stark, uncomfortable reality, but God's people have not changed all that much over the years.

Brothers and sisters, now is the time. Now is the time for us to put aside our rebellion, tear down the idols in our lives, forgive and love each other as Christ commanded, and answer once again to the King of Kings and Lord of Lords. He is faithful and just to forgive, and He is waiting with open arms to rescue and redeem us. But in order for Him to do so, we must turn away from our own wicked ways and turn toward Him. He is our Savior and our King and we owe Him our very lives. If we will offer them to Him in love and obedient submission, He will take all that appears to be hopeless and impossible and bring from it beauty and redemption beyond anything we can ask or imagine. Glory be to our God and King!

True Righteousness and Holiness

You were taught, with regard to your former way of life, to put off
your old self, which is being corrupted by its deceitful desires; to
be made new in the attitude of your minds; and to put on the new
self, created to be like God in true righteousness and holiness.
—Ephesians 4:22–24

If anyone is in Christ, he is a new creation: The old has
gone, the new is here! All this is from God, who reconciled
us to himself through Christ and gave us the ministry of
reconciliation. ... We are therefore Christ's ambassadors,
as though God were making his appeal through us. ...
God made him who had no sin to be sin for us, so that
in him we might become the righteousness of God.
—2 Corinthians 5:17–18, 20–21

When we surrender our lives to Christ and invite Him to be our Savior
and King, He sets us free from sin and literally gives us a new self; we
become new creations. The purpose of that new self is tucked away
in Ephesians 4:24: to be like God in true righteousness and holiness.
If that is God's proclaimed primary reason, we need to realize and
trust that everything He does, everything He allows us to go through,
every attack He allows Satan to inflict, every tear, struggle, trial and
hardship that we face, is in our lives as His Craftsman's tool to shape
and refine us to that end. He uses all of it to a grander end than we
could imagine, producing in us true righteousness and holiness that
matches His! Take a moment to consider that, because it should
impact the way we look at every difficulty or trial that comes our
way. As long as we work in concert with God and remain submitted
in His hand and trusting His ways, He will use absolutely everything,

everything, we go through to grow us into far more than we could ever be on our own. May we trust the artistry of God's hand!

This world is lost. Everywhere you turn, you see evidence of overwhelming evil, pain and suffering. Wherever you are as you read this, you are no doubt in contact with people who are spiritually dead and are in desperate need for hope and salvation. We need to start living as the new creations God made us. We have been reconciled to Christ, and because of that reconciliation, we are now God's ambassadors. God is making His appeal to this lost and dying world through us. Cast off who you used to be, the chains and snares that used to entangle you, and allow God to shine His light and love through you. You are His voice, His hands, His feet. Through you He calls out to the world with a plea to allow Him to rescue and redeem. Ask yourself, what message of God is my life proclaiming? God, help us be like You in true righteousness and holiness.

God's Temple

When Jesus entered the temple courts, he began to drive out those who were selling. "It is written," he said to them. "'My house will be a house of prayer', but you have made it a 'den of robbers.'"
—Luke 19:45–46

Don't you know that you yourselves are God's temple
and that God's Spirit dwells in your midst?
—I Corinthians 3:16

Do you not know that your bodies are a temple of the
Holy Spirit, who is in you, whom you have received
from God? You are not your own; you were bought at
a price. Therefore honor God with your bodies.
—I Corinthians 6:19–20

The day you received Jesus Christ as your Savior, He came to live inside you through the Holy Spirit. Your body became His home, His dwelling place, His temple. In biblical times, God's temple was a structure. It was a building that was intended to be a place of worship and sacrifice to God Most High. With the gift of the indwelling Holy Spirit, we no longer have to go to a man-made building to be in the midst of God's presence. His presence is in us. However, just like the temple structure frequently became defiled and full of corruption, so too do our bodies, which include our hearts and minds.

Take a moment to examine the state of God's temple, your body. Consider the words that pour forth from it. Are they words that build up and express love, or words that tear down and express bitterness and hatred? Consider the actions that derive from it. Are they actions of service, self-giving, and helping those in need, or are they actions of greed and ignoring those in need? What sort of things do you allow to enter into it? Do you invite in things and people that point you toward Christ and encourage you to worship Him, grow in Him and surrender to Him, or do you allow in things and people that pull you away from Christ, that tempt you to acts of self-gratification and chasing after the things of this world? Who is worshipped in the temple? Is it truly God's temple, or has it become full of idols who have stolen your devotion away from God and been seated on the throne in His rightful place?

The reality is that if we do not daily take stock of God's temple in us, if we do not daily examine our hearts, minds, actions, and motives, the temple will become defiled. Worship of God will be replaced with worship of self. Thoughts of God and what pleases Him will be replaced with thoughts of self and what pleases us. We need to ask God to examine us, to inspect His temple within us, and to reveal any rooms where corruption has taken root, any areas where defilement resides. We need to surrender our entire selves to Him and allow Him to purge from us anything that displeases Him. We are not our own. Our bodies, our hearts, our minds are not our own. We have been bought by the priceless blood of Jesus Christ. His Spirit dwells in us. May He be honored and glorified in His temple.

Witnesses

You will receive power when the Holy Spirit comes on
you; and you will be my witnesses in Jerusalem, and in
all Judea and Samaria, and to the ends of the earth.
—Acts 1:8

In the same way, let your light shine before others, that they
may see your good deeds and glorify your Father in heaven.
—Matthew 5:16

But we have this treasure in jars of clay to show that this
all-surpassing power is from God and not from us.
—2 Corinthians 4:7

Therefore, if anyone is in Christ, the new creation has
come: The old has gone, the new is here!
—2 Corinthians 5:17

What does your life attest to? If someone were to observe your life for a time, what would they witness? If he or she knew nothing about you, knew nothing of your profession to be a follower of Christ, would that person conclude just by watching you that there is something markedly different about you? Through observing your actions, your attitudes, and your responses to difficult or challenging situations, would that person see someone who is marked by grace and love?

If someone was to watch you go through a time of uncertainty, would he or she see someone unusually calm and at peace? If that person saw you being mistreated or wronged, would he or she see someone respond not out of anger and retaliation but out of love and forgiveness? Would he or she walk away curious about what makes you so different? Would that person's mind be stirred to discover what your secret is? Or would he or she see a life that blends in with all the others—a life that is just as fearful, doubtful, selfish, and unsatisfied as the rest of the world? Would that person walk away concluding that you are no different than anyone else?

Through God's plan, He chose to use us as His witnesses to a dying world. His intention is for those who are saved by His grace to be transformed into a new creation. Our lives are to be so filled by the light of the Holy Spirit that we shine in the darkness as a beacon, drawing those caught in the crushing storm of sin to the shores of God's love and salvation. Our lives are to increasingly resemble the likeness of Christ. What is so amazing about God's design is that He knows we are frail jars of clay, inevitably prone to cracking and imperfections. It would seem that His plan is flawed, that surely He could have chosen a better way to show Himself to the world.

And yet, even in what at first appears to be faulty planning, He demonstrates His wisdom. For it is because of our frailties and our inabilities to save ourselves that He is able to exhibit His glory through us. We have no other explanation for peace, for love, for strength in times of weakness and grace in times of pain, than God's transforming love and power in our lives. It is truly when we are weak that He most shows His strength. It is when we admit our inability to do "it," whatever "it" is at any given moment, that He steps in and displays His amazing grace and sovereignty.

But catch that, because we have a responsibility in it. We must admit that we cannot do life on our own. We have to admit that we are not strong enough, good enough, or smart enough. When we fail to acknowledge that and instead attempt to plow through life with our own grit, we become bitter, burned out, and anxious. We become the envious observers of people who exhibit peace and calm and wonder why we do not have that. You can! Simply bring yourself back to the feet of the Lord and admit your frailty to Him. Allow Him to fill your cracked pot with His peace and love, and you will find that it is through those cracks that He is shining, beckoning a dying world to life.

Be His witness. Be His evidence of transformation. Allow Him to achieve His plan through you, and your life will undoubtedly stir curiosity in those who observe it.

Let It Be as You Say

"I am the LORD's servant," Mary answered.
"May your word to me be fulfilled."
—Luke 1:38

[The LORD's] pleasure is not in the strength of the horse, nor
his delight in the legs of the warrior; the LORD delights in those
who fear him, who put their hope in his unfailing love.
—Psalm 147:10–11

We are likely all familiar with the story of Gabriel visiting Mary, proclaiming that she has been chosen by God to bear His Son. We know the story of the journey she and Joseph took that led them to a stable in Bethlehem where Mary gave birth to Jesus. We all know the Christmas story and about the shepherds and angels and wise men, and the star that led them all to Jesus' feet. But I would like to take a moment to pause and consider Mary's response to the news before the plan began to unfold.

Mary had just been told that her entire world was about to be flipped upside down. The role God had chosen her for was no minor thing. She was young and unmarried, and she lived in a time when pregnancy out of wedlock was punishable by stoning. She was engaged to a man who believed her to be innocent and pure, and somehow she needed to tell him she was pregnant, both of them knowing it was not his child.

Upon hearing God's calling for her, Mary could have gotten angry, could have demanded an explanation, and could have even refused to believe it was truly from God, because it did not make sense and it did not align with how the world says life should go. But she did not respond in any of those ways. Instead, she declared herself to be God's servant and simply said, "Let it be as you say." She did not kick, she did not grumble, and she did not storm off. She submitted. She laid down all of her own plans for her life, her own desires and will and even her reputation, and she accepted God's plan. Although Jesus was yet to be conceived in her womb, she already had room in herself for Him. Her heart and her mind were already prepared for His will and ways.

God calls each of us in much the same way as He called Mary. He has a life that He wants to breathe into us, a life provided through His Son, Jesus Christ. As with Mary, this new life offers hope and salvation, but it also involves our lives being turned upside down. It will involve letting go of our own plans and preconceived ideas of how life should go, and choosing to submit our wills, our desires, and even our reputations to God's plan.

Through us, God desires to share His Son with every person we encounter. Through us, He wants to proclaim that the Savior of the world has been born to redeem and to save. In order for Him to accomplish that purpose, we must be as Mary was. We must have room in our hearts for God. We must be pliable in His hands, allowing Him to bend and shape every part of who we are and what our lives look like in whatever ways He chooses. That kind of submission flows from a heart that trusts its God. That kind of servitude pours from a hope that is founded upon God's unfailing love. That kind of trust and willingness to accept God's plan, no matter how counterintuitive or uncertain it seems, is the fruit of a life that rests in God's unending goodness and wisdom.

Look at the amazing blessing Mary received by bending her knee and saying yes to God's plan. She was mother to the Savior of the world! Choose to learn from her example. Say to the Lord, "Let it be as you say." Offer yourself to Him as His servant, choosing to trust your entire being to His love and purpose. Allow Him to be born in you and then share that Life with the whole world!

God's Vessels

The fruit of the Spirit is love, joy, peace, forbearance, kindness, goodness, faithfulness, gentleness and self-control. Against such things there is no law.
—Galatians 5:22–23

Love is patient, love is kind. It does not envy, it does not boast, it is not proud. It does not dishonor others, it is not self-seeking, it is not easily angered, it keeps no record of wrongs. Love does not delight in evil but rejoices with the truth. It always protects, always trusts, always hopes, always perseveres.
—I Corinthians 13:4–7

The call of each of our lives in Christ is to be God's vessel. Consider the function of a vessel. It contains and it pours out. A vessel holds what is necessary until that which it contains is poured out for a purpose. So too our lives are intended to contain and to pour out.

What are we intended to contain? The Holy Spirit first and foremost. When we accept Christ as our Savior, the Holy Spirit fills us and becomes our witness of salvation, the seal indicating we have been redeemed. He fills us with all that we need in order to live a life of faith and continually grow closer to God. We contain the peace of God that transcends understanding, His love that transforms us and turns our hearts of stone into hearts of flesh, and we are equipped with all that we need to stand firm against the enemy and persevere to accomplish God's purpose for our lives. As God's vessels, we should be filled with all that pleases Him.

What then should our lives be pouring out? Everywhere we go, with every person we encounter and every situation we face, our lives should be pouring out evidence of the Holy Spirit, which shows itself through love. Love expresses itself through joy, peace, patience, kindness, goodness, faithfulness, gentleness, and self-control. In every moment of our lives, God's love should be pouring out and spilling into this world. Our lives should emit a love that this world cannot explain and that causes it to realize what depravity there is without such love. Our lives should overflow with Jesus's healing water, beckoning all who are dying of thirst to come to Him and drink.

Unfortunately, that is rarely the case. More often than not, our lives are not free-flowing vessels that exude God so completely. Rather, we are riddled with debris and sludge that hinders the flow and cakes the walls of our vessels, limiting both what we are able to contain and what we are able to pour out. We become coated in a grime of worry, fear, bitterness, hatred, selfishness, and impatience. Those impurities limit our abilities to live full of the Holy Spirit, and pollute that which flows from us, creating a hindered dribble that fails to bring life to the dying.

Continually examine the state of your vessel. Search that which is hidden in you. Does the Holy Spirit have access to transform and fill every part of your life, or are there portions that are caked with debris and blocked off from Him? Take stock of that which pours forth from your life. Does it bear the fruit of God's love and offer patience, kindness and gentleness? Or is it polluted with things which cause those who are touched by it to feel unloved, unwanted, and pushed out of the way? As you walk this journey with God, ask Him to purify you more and more until at last He has a vessel which He can fill to the brim and through which He can pour out His love and grace in overflowing abundance.

Whom Shall I Send?

In the year that King Uzziah died, I saw the Lord, high and
exalted, seated on a throne; and the train of his robe filled the
temple. Above him were seraphim, each with six wings: With two
wings they covered their faces, with two they covered their feet, and
with two they were flying. And they were calling to one another:
"Holy, holy, holy is the LORD Almighty;
the whole earth is full of his glory."
At the sound of their voices the doorposts and thresholds
shook and the temple was filled with smoke.
"Woe to me!" I cried. "I am ruined! For I am a man of
unclean lips, and I live among a people of unclean lips,
and my eyes have seen the King, the LORD Almighty."
Then one of the seraphim flew to me with a live coal in his
hand, which he had taken with tongs from the altar. With it
he touched my mouth and said, "See, this has touched your
lips; your guilt is taken away and your sin atoned for."
Then I heard the voice of the Lord saying, "Whom
shall I send? And who will go for us?"
And I said, "Here am I. Send me!"
—Isaiah 6:1–8

God extends the invitation for us to be participants in His plan. He
seeks for someone who is willing and wanting to go for Him, to live
for Him. He does not *need* us; He *invites* us. Think of that—the God
of all creation, who is all-powerful and all-knowing, the sustainer of
all things, wants us to join Him in His purpose and plans! What an
amazing honor!

However, we do not receive that invitation because of our own
merit or qualifications. The invitation follows key steps that must
first be completed, and those steps can be found in the story of

Isaiah's commission. The story begins with the Lord revealing Himself to Isaiah. He meets Isaiah where he is and Isaiah comes face to face with the glory, splendor, and majesty of the Lord. He is confronted with the holiness of God and the power of His name. When Isaiah sees Him and recognizes who he has just encountered, his response is complete and utter humility. He is instantly aware of his unworthiness to stand before the Lord, and Isaiah confesses that he is sinful and possesses no goodness in and of himself.

So too it is for us when we are first wooed by the Lord when He first reveals Himself to us and leads us into His presence. When we encounter this Holy God, we cannot help but fall to our knees in stark awareness of our utter unholiness. In the light of His glory and perfection, we see with clear eyes our own darkness and sinfulness.

Following Isaiah's confession of God as King and himself as unworthy, he is then touched and forgiven. His guilt is removed, and his sins are atoned for. By recognizing and confessing his sinfulness and depravity, he opens himself up to receive forgiveness and redemption. Once again, the same is true for us. When we come to that place where we recognize and confess that we are broken, sinful, and in need of a Savior, we open the door for Jesus to enter in and remove our guilt and sin. He is the great atonement, who washes us with His blood and declares us forgiven and cleansed.

It is after that, after recognizing and declaring who God is and being washed of our sins, that God extends the invitation. Just as with Isaiah, He seeks men and women today who are willing to be sent by Him to speak His word and share His love. He searches for men and women who desire to be a part of His purpose and who want to be instruments and tools in the Craftsman's hands. He calls out to each of His children, asking who will trust Him enough, obey Him enough, and surrender to Him enough to offer themselves as active participants in His plans.

Notice He does not tell Isaiah what the role will entail ahead of time, nor does He do so with us. He does not lay out the map and let us look at the game plan before we make our decision. He simply asks, "Whom shall I send?" Will you respond to that call as Isaiah did? Will your whole-hearted response be, "Here am I. Send me!"?

If you are willing to say yes, even without knowing the details of the plans, God will use you in ways you could never imagine to accomplish a purpose you could never have dreamed. The author of life will include you in His story and lead you to participate in His plan to rescue and redeem the lost and dying so they too can be touched by Jesus and healed. Every day God presents the invitation, and every day we make a choice whether to say yes or to say no. Today, every day, say yes to Him. It will be a yes that impacts eternity.

CHAPTER 3

FAITH AND TRUST

In The Waiting

We boast in the hope of the glory of God. Not only so,
but we also glory in our sufferings, because we know that
suffering produces perseverance; perseverance, character;
and character, hope. And hope does not put us to shame,
because God's love has been poured out into our hearts
through the Holy Spirit, who has been given to us.
—Romans 5:2–5

And we know that in all things God works for the good of those
who love him, who have been called according to his purpose.
—Romans 8:28

I remain confident of this: I will see the goodness of
the LORD in the land of the living. Wait for the LORD;
be strong and take heart and wait for the LORD.
—Psalm 27:13–14

Every single one of us has a "thing" in our lives—a specific area or
aspect of our lives that we long for or wish would change but has not
yet come to fruition. For some it is finding a mate, for others it is
having a child, and for others it is a change of profession or restored
health or a desire for a new beginning in life. Whatever it is, we each
carry in us an aspect of our lives that we long for. The process of
receiving that desired thing involves an unavoidable element for each
one of us—waiting. We pray, we ask God to clear the way and grant
our desire, and yet inevitably after praying, we all must wait.

Sometimes the waiting is brief (although we would never say so at
the time). Sometimes the waiting is longer, but let us be honest—in
our impatient human nature, waiting an *hour* is too long. And so we
bring our desires before God, place them at His feet and ask for His

guidance and blessing in it, and more often than not proceed to tap our foot and watch the clock, expecting that surely He will not delay "too" long.

The problem is we become so focused on the waiting that we miss what God is doing in it. And He *is* active in it. In fact, it is in that place of surrender and dependence on Him, when we do not have the natural ability to make the circumstances change in and of ourselves, that we have the opportunity to grow and develop more than potentially any other time in our lives. Dependence on God and waiting upon Him develops faith, trust, perseverance, self-sacrifice, hope, and a firm confidence in the nature and character of the God on whom we rely.

However, notice I said we have the *opportunity* to grow and develop in those times; it does not happen automatically or without our active participation in the process. More often than not, what happens in those times, which stunts our growth and inhibits any development of our faith and trust in God, is that we shrink God down to the size of the obstacle we face so that in our minds they become equal "opponents." If we allow ourselves to take our eyes off God and His character, His promises of faithfulness, and His vow to work all things together for our good, we begin to see the obstacle as being too big to move and God too small to move it. We minimize God and His sovereignty and fear that He is not strong enough, not wise enough, simply not *enough*, to make a way.

The truth is, God is way bigger, way stronger, and way more powerful than anything that we face in our lives. He is not to be measured by the perceived size of the obstacle. Instead the obstacle should be viewed in light of who God is. Nothing is impossible for Him. He calls the sun to rise and to set every single day, He holds together every ligament and fiber of our bodies, He knows every star in every galaxy by name. Even the demons are subject to His majesty and rule. Nothing we face is too big for our God. Nothing we desire is too hard for Him to grant.

So as you are waiting on Him for whatever that "thing" is in your life, seize the opportunity to grow and develop here and now, in the waiting. He has a glorious future planned for you beyond your imagination. But as you hope in Him for that future, be sure to maintain a proper perspective of the size of the obstacle compared to the immeasurable power of your God. He is not silent. He has not forgotten you. He is using all of this for your good, even the waiting.

Certain of What We Cannot See

When the servant of the man of God got up and went out
early the next morning, an army with horses and chariots had
surrounded the city. "Oh no, my lord! What shall we do?" the
servant asked. "Don't be afraid," the prophet answered. "Those
who are with us are more than those who are with them." And
Elisha prayed, "Open his eyes, LORD, so that he may see." Then
the LORD opened the servant's eyes, and he looked and saw the
hills full of horses and chariots of fire all around Elisha.
—2 Kings 6:15–17

I will lead the blind by ways they have not known, along
unfamiliar paths I will guide them; I will turn the darkness
into light before them and make the rough places smooth.
There are the things I will do; I will not forsake them.
—Isaiah 42:16

What do you do when God does not make sense? What do you do
when you cannot see His answer to prayers, when you cannot see what
He is doing? In every believer's life those times are inevitable. In fact,
the walk of faith is more frequently mark with times of blindness
than times of sight. Faith is not believing in things seen; it is being
certain of things we *do not* see. The reality of every Christian's life is
that God leads us down paths for which He does not give us a map
ahead of time. We are each called to follow Him, one step at a time,
even when we are blind to what He is doing and where He is leading
us. The key is to not allow ourselves to be distracted and consumed
by our lack of sight. Our natural selves want to wrestle and strive for
knowing all the turns and bends ahead of time. Our natural selves
resist the idea of walking blindly, and much more prefer to walk by
fact and self-reliance than by trust and God-reliance. However, as

children of God, we are no longer to be ruled by our sinful natures. The moment we became His, He set out to refine us, break us free from the restrictions and cage of the natural, and lead us into the freedom and glory of the eternal.

If we allow ourselves to focus on our own perceptions and sight, or lack thereof, we will inevitably become consumed by doubt and fear. We will believe the lie that because we cannot see what God is doing it means He is not doing anything at all. In 2 Kings 6:15, that is what Elisha's servant was facing. His natural self only saw the enemy surrounding them on every side, and to him all seemed hopeless. However, all was not as it appeared. In response to Elisha's prayer, God opened the servant's eyes to see that they were not alone in the battle. God's own heavenly army was there with them, protecting them. The servant's inability to see God's deliverance did not make it any less real.

Hang on in this time of blindness. Continue on down this path of faith. Even when you cannot see Him, God is with you. He will turn your darkness into light; He will level the path under your feet. Continue allowing Him to break you out of the restrictions of the natural and release you into the glory of the eternal. Though you cannot see, God can. Though you do not understand, God does. Trust His hand holding yours and keep following Him. He will never leave you on your own.

Face the Impossible

When Daniel was lifted from the den, no wound was
found on him, because he had trusted in his God.
—Daniel 6:23

[The Reubenites, the Gadites and the half-tribe of Manasseh] were
helped in fighting them, and God delivered the Hagrites and all
their allies over to them, because they cried out to [God] during the
battle. He answered their prayers, because they had trusted in Him.
—I Chronicles 5:20

The LORD will fight for you; you need only to be still.
—Exodus 14:14

God loves "impossible" situations. Take a look at Moses or Gideon,
Elijah or David, just to name a few. Take a look at situations God's
people so often find themselves in, against enemies that appear
indestructible, walls that appear insurmountable. Time and time
again, God orchestrates circumstances in which any hope of victory
or success seems ludicrous and ridiculous. He calls His child to step
on to the battlefield and face the enemy, and then trust God for a
seemingly impossible victory. Oftentimes, we read about these stories
and battles in the Bible, and we tend to gloss over how difficult they
were, how impossible they seemed, because we have the benefit of
knowing how the story ends. However, those were actual people,
feeble, scared sinners just like us, facing those situations that brought
them face to face with the possibility of death. They did not know
how the story would end but they chose to trust God to fight for
them regardless.

God calls us to that same trust and confidence in Him. When
we respond to that call, when we put our faith into action and not

just claim to trust God but actually exercise that trust, He will bring about the victory, and no foe can prevail against Him. He will move mountains and split seas for the child who puts his or her faith to work. Today, examine your hearts. Quiet yourselves before God and listen. There is undoubtedly something He is calling you to do, something for which He is beckoning you to put your faith in Him. Rise up and respond. Put your faith into action and watch what your God will do.

Faith and Deeds

Someone will say, "You have faith; I have deeds." Show me your faith without deeds, and I will show you my faith by my deeds. You believe that there is one God. Good! Even the demons believe that—and shudder. You foolish person, do you want evidence that faith without deeds is useless? Was not our father Abraham considered righteous for what he did when he offered his son Isaac on the altar? You see that his faith and his actions were working together, and his faith was made complete by what he did. And the scripture was fulfilled that says, "Abraham believed God, and it was credited to him as righteousness," and he was called God's friend. You see that a person is considered righteous by what they do and not by faith alone. In the same way, was not even Rahab the prostitute considered righteous for what she did when she gave lodging to the spies and sent them off in a different direction? As the body without the spirit is dead, so faith without deeds is dead.
—James 2:18–26

Now faith is confidence in what we hope for and assurance about what we do not see. ... And without faith it is impossible to please God, because anyone who comes to him must believe that he exists and that he rewards those who earnestly seek him.
—Hebrews 11:1, 6

Belief and faith are not the same thing. To say we believe God exists is not the same as declaring that our faith is in Him. James 4:19 makes this very clear by stating that even demons acknowledge there is one God. So what sets a Christian apart? What is the distinction that marks a life lived in faith? In one word, *action*. Our lives in Christ must be expressed through faith in action, faith that not only believes God is real but also takes Him at His word and follows Him accordingly.

Oftentimes, though, that action does not express itself in the ways we typically think it would. When we hear or are told to put our faith into action, it frequently means to take a step, do a thing, and trust that God will catch you if you fall. Action here means something different. Faith in action means exercising our confidence and firm stance to listen for, wait on, and watch for God to move, answer, and clear the path in His way and timing. In Hebrews 11, faith is defined as being sure of what is hoped for and certain of what is not yet seen. But then it goes a step further and states that without faith it is impossible to please God because anyone who comes to Him must believe that He exists and that He rewards those who earnestly seek Him. Believing that He rewards those who seek Him is *faith*. Choosing to step out and follow Him even when you cannot see the full path ahead of you is *faith*. Standing still when He tells you to wait rather than rushing ahead in your own plans is *faith*. Responding to His call to pray that He will bring victory in a battle you face, and then trusting and expecting Him to, is *faith*. Faith challenges us to consider the heart and character of God and cling to His countless, amazing promises to His children. He cannot fail, He will not disappoint, and He rewards those who earnestly seek Him. Those are God's own words about Himself and He cannot lie.

May our lives be marked by faith in action, a faith that is living and breathing, a faith that resounds from each of our lives, even without words. May the world look at us and see something different, something that emulates the living, loving, powerful God that we serve.

God of Mystery

*My goal is that they may be encouraged in heart and united in love,
so that they may have the full riches of complete understanding, in
order that they may know the mystery of God, namely, Christ, in
whom are hidden all the treasures of wisdom and knowledge.*
—Colossians 2:2-3

There are many stages throughout each Christian's walk with God.
He is continually changing, shaping, and challenging us to grow
deeper, draw closer, and live more wholly for Him. Some of the stages
are exciting and joyful, when we feel closer to God than ever before.
We feel Him with us, we can see and hear Him in new ways, and we
feel ready to take on the world.

Then there are other stages, stages that bring us to our knees in
wonder of His sovereignty and holiness when He allows us glimpses
of how awesome He is. We long to worship and praise Him and be
caught up in awe of Him.

Then there is another stage, a stage in which we do not feel
Him. We do not see or hear Him more than ever before. We do not
see tangible displays of His mighty working hand. Instead, we find
ourselves shrouded, confronted with the reality that God is a God
of mystery. We beg and plead to know what He is doing, what the
purpose of the moment is. We ask Him to reveal Himself (typically
in ways we want Him to), and to remind us of how much He loves us.
We beg to feel Him, for reassurance that He is still here. Sometimes,
however, His answer to those requests is no. He may choose not to
fill us in on what He's doing in that moment. He may choose not to
reveal what purposes He is using us for in that time and place. He
may choose not to speak or wrap us up in cozy blankets so we are
coddled and reassured. He may instead choose to show us that He

is a God of mystery who is teaching us that He is set apart and holy and far bigger than we will ever be able to understand.

We like to romanticize mystery, but the truth of the matter is it makes us uncomfortable. If we are scared, we want reassurance that it is safe. If we are confused, we want to be given clarity so we can make sense of what we are facing. However, that is not always what we need, despite it being what we want. If we truly want to know God more, if we really want to grow deeper in our relationship with Him, then at times we need to experience Him as a God mystery. We need to let the mystery surround us and learn to remain in it, trusting that He is still the God we know Him to be.

Unconditional

"For my thoughts are not your thoughts, neither are
your ways my ways," declares the LORD. "As the heavens
are higher than the earth, so are my ways higher than
your ways and my thoughts than your thoughts."
—Isaiah 55:8–9

For you have been my hope, Sovereign LORD,
my confidence since my youth.
—Psalm 71:5

Therefore we do not lose heart. Though outwardly we are
wasting away, yet inwardly we are being renewed day by day.
—2 Corinthians 4:16

Is your relationship with God conditional? That is a very bold, uncomfortable question, but take a moment to truly consider it. Your love, obedience, trust, surrender, even your hope and joy in Him—are those things conditional at times, based on what He does or does not do, how He seemingly does or does not answer your prayers?

Our initial reaction is of course to say no, that is never true of us. But let us be truly honest with ourselves. There are times in our walks of faith when we wrestle with God, times when He does not answer how or when we want Him to, or maybe it seems He is not answering at all and we are tempted to give up. There are times when He seems silent or indifferent or as if He is not holding up His end of the deal.

In those times, what is our reaction? Do we continue to trust, stay surrendered, maintain our hope and confidence in Him, or do we consider doing things our own way, following our own plans? I will be transparent enough to confess that I wrestle with those things at times, and I do not imagine I am the only one. When He does not do things the way I think is best, I battle with frustration toward Him.

However, the Holy Spirit confronts me in those moments and asks, "When you surrendered your life to Christ and turned everything over to Him, asking for His will above all else, did you put conditions on it? Did you say, 'You can have it all, as long as I understand the plan and it goes along with what I want when I want it.'"

Of course I did not; when I fell on my knees before Him and asked Him to rescue me, I was fully aware that my own attempts at life and decision-making only led to regrets, destruction and death. I knew that I desperately needed a Savior and that all hope, grace, and life were found only in Him. I handed my all over to Him, choosing Him and His plans over my own, unequivocally.

I think sometimes we need to return to that moment of surrender in our minds when we recognized that He is the only way and only answer. When you struggle to maintain trust in God and His ways and you are tempted to believe that you know better than He does, ask yourself if you are allowing conditions to dictate your relationship with Him. When you do not understand—will you trust Him? When His answers seem delayed—will you trust Him? When His ways do not seem to make sense—will you trust Him?

Remember that this God who you are following, the One who you have surrendered your life to, loves you *unconditionally*. There is nothing you did to deserve it; there is nothing you can do to lose it. He loved you before you took your first breath. In those seasons and moments when you are tempted to lose heart, tempted to measure your trust and walk with Him by what you can see and understand, remember that He who loves you beyond comprehension has your absolute best interest in mind. He can be trusted, followed, hoped in *unconditionally*. He will never love you with less than His absolute best, and so He will only ever lead you to the absolute best.

He Is Faithful

For the word of the LORD is right and
true; he is faithful in all he does.
—Psalm 33:4

If we died with him, we will also live with him;
If we endure, we will also reign with him;
If we disown him, he will also disown us;
If we are faithless, he will remain faithful,
for he cannot disown himself.
—2 Timothy 2:11–13

This morning during my quiet time I was reading through the Psalms, and I was struck by the fourth verse of chapter thirty-three, specifically the line "he is faithful in all he does." As I considered those words, I started examining and challenging myself with some sobering reflections. I found myself in a place of both humility and awe, recognizing and confessing areas of weakness in my faith while at the same time being overwhelmed by what an amazing, loving, faithful God we serve. As you consider the following reflections, perhaps you too will be challenged to confess areas of weakness and declare God's faithfulness. Only He can cut right to the heart of our frailties and expose areas still darkened by our sinful natures while at the same time flooding us with wave upon wave of unconditional love and grace that covers over all our sins. Thank God He does not leave us as we are.

God's faithfulness is not dependent on whether or not I believe He is always faithful. He is not on trial before me. I am not judge and jury, gathering up what I deem to be evidence of whether or not God is faithful and then from that declaring my own verdict of whether or not He is. (I make that distinction of what I deem to be evidence because the truth of the matter is we are surrounded all the time by evidence of His unfailing faithfulness. Oftentimes we turn a blind eye to them but they are always there.) He *is* always faithful, whether I choose to believe it or not. And truly, who am I to argue against Him? Who am I to challenge His claim and search for contradictory proof? And perhaps worst of all, who am I to receive blessing and mercy every moment of every day *because* of His faithfulness and yet still at times withhold my trust that He is and always will be faithful? He is God; I am not. I would do well to remember that next time I consider sitting as judge over His character.

In All That You Do

So whether you eat or drink or whatever you
do, do it all for the glory of God.
—I Corinthians 10:31

Though the fig tree does not bud and there are no grapes on
the vines, though the olive crop fails and the fields produce no
food, though there are no sheep in the pen and no cattle in the
stalls, yet I will rejoice in the Lord, I will be joyful in God my
Savior. The Sovereign Lord is my strength; he makes my feet
like the feet of a deer, he enables me to tread on the heights.
—Habakkuk 3:17-19

Let's face it—there are times on this walk of faith when life is not
a mountaintop experience. We are not always discovering new and
exciting things, we do not always feel closer to God than ever before,
and we are not always privy to the things God is doing. Certainly those
mountaintop moments happen, and we are filled with encouragement
and renewed enthusiasm during them. But that is not where most of
life is lived. The majority of life is spent below the mountaintop, on
the path that weaves and turns through level plains, through the midst
of the day-to-day routine. It is likely that if someone were to ask us
how our day was, our most common answer would be something
along the lines of "It was a typical day."

In general, people do not like "typical." We crave those
mountaintop experiences, and easily we become discouraged and
maybe even pessimistic when we are not in the midst of one. We
have a bad habit of looking around at our daily lives and feeling
discontented and disgruntled by what we do (or do not) see. We
generally have a picture in our minds of where our lives should be
going and feel that we should be getting there *now*, and when we find

ourselves in the same circumstances without sensing any change, we can easily become embittered and resentful.

However, God never said life would be a continuous mountaintop experience. He never promised excitement and bliss at every turn. In fact, the Bible is full of evidence that life is not easy, it is not always exciting, and it will not always go exactly as we had hoped or planned. So what are we to do? When we rise in the morning to the same responsibilities and duties that we had yesterday, what should our response be? The Bible in I Corinthians 10:31 makes it clear: "So whether you eat or drink or whatever you do, do it all for the glory of God."

Whatever you do, do it all for the glory of God. So when you get up in the morning to go to the same job you had yesterday, when you are driving along the same commute you take multiple times a week, when you are grabbing something to eat at a local restaurant, when you are interacting with those around you, do it all for the glory of God. If we could begin to live every moment of our lives with that at the forefront of our minds, do you know what would happen? There would be no typical moments. There would be no monotony in our routines. Every task we go about would become an opportunity to honor God. We would wake up each morning with the realization that the day is brimming with potential to glorify our Savior.

Habakkuk takes that challenge a step further. It is not just about praising and honoring God in the day-to-day normalcy of life. He prompts us to be joyful even when things are going badly, times when, rather than being on top of the mountain, we are deep down in the valley being challenged with difficulty and strife. Even at those times, when it would seem there is no cause for rejoicing, when it seems ridiculous to be joyful, even then we have cause to praise God and bring Him glory. For truly He is our strength, even when all else fails. He is the one who enables us to rise each day and face whatever may come.

Today, make the choice to begin seeing each moment as an opportunity to bring glory to God. Live your life with eyes wide open, seeking to recognize and take advantage of the incredible potential every breath holds. Smile, listen, lift your gaze to the beauty of your surroundings. Do not just look at the people around you but see them. In all that you do, seek to have the eyes, ears, heart, and mind of Christ, and aspire to respond and live as He did. If that becomes our daily mission, we will truly bring glory to God in all that we do.

God's Presence

Do not worry about your life, what you will eat or drink; or about
your body, what you will wear. Is not life more than food, and
the body more than clothes? Look at the birds of the air; they
do not sow or reap or store away in barns, and yet your heavenly
Father feeds them. Are you not much more valuable than they?
Can any one of you by worrying add a single hour to your life?
And why do you worry about clothes? See how the flowers of the
field grow. They do not labor or spin. Yet I tell you that not even
Solomon in all his splendor was dressed like one of these. If that
is how God clothes the grass of the field, which is here today and
tomorrow is thrown into the fire, will he not much more clothe
you—you of little faith? So do not worry, saying, "What shall we
eat?" or "What shall we drink?" or "What shall we wear?" For
the pagans run after all these things, and your heavenly Father
knows that you need them. But seek first his kingdom and his
righteousness, and all these things will be given to you as well.
Therefore do not worry about tomorrow, for tomorrow will
worry about itself. Each day has enough trouble of its own.
—Matthew 6:25–34

Whether you turn to the right or to the left, your ears will hear
a voice behind you, saying, "This is the way; walk in it."
—Isaiah 30:21

There is nothing in your life that goes unnoticed by God. To take it a
step further, there is nothing in your life by which God is surprised or
caught off guard. He is not a stranger to your difficulties or unaware
of the decisions that you face. In fact, not only is He aware of all
the details of your life, but also He knows the purpose behind all
of them. So often we think of God as distant or someone we need

to make aware of what we face, but the reality is He knows your life better than you do. He knows the right choice in every decision and the solution to every problem. We typically look at the obstacle we face and wonder if God is big enough to overcome it. Instead, what we ought to do is recognize what God is doing in the midst of the obstacle.

There is nothing we face in this life that God does not intend to use for our eternal glory if we will just invite Him into it and ask Him to open our eyes to His will and His ways. In every challenge, every victory, every beginning, and every end, God intends to draw us deeper into relationship with Him. He desires to cultivate deeper trust, authentic faith, and freedom from our self-will and self-love so we can live in the glory and rest of His will and love.

When we face uncertain times, when someone close to us betrays us, when things seem to be unraveling all around us, the question to ask is not, "God, where are You in this?" What we should be asking is, "God, what are You trying to teach me in this and where does Your hand want to lead me?" In all things, at all times, He is right there beside us. That is truth, whether we acknowledge His presence or not. But what heartache we cause Him and needless struggle and despair we cause ourselves when we ignore His presence!

We need to move past the place of infantile faith, asking God to prove His faithfulness and presence in our lives, and begin living in light of and conviction of unshakeable faith that He *is*. We need to approach everything we face in our lives with the awareness that if God allowed it, He must have a divine purpose for it. Our aim and pursuit needs to not be for the easy road free from trouble, but for the heart of God and living in His presence in all things. Do not miss His glorious intention for this moment, this day. He is here and He wants to lead you into things not yet seen.

The Marked-Out Race

Therefore, since we are surrounded by such a great cloud
of witnesses, let us throw off everything that hinders and the
sin that so easily entangles. And let us run with perseverance
the race marked out for us, fixing our eyes on Jesus, the pioneer
and perfecter of faith. For the joy set before him he endured
the cross, scorning its shame, and sat down at the right hand of
the throne of God. Consider him who endured such opposition
from sinners, so that you will not grow weary and lose heart.
—Hebrews 12:1–3

In order for a race to be marked out, someone had to first go ahead
of the runners and map it out. Someone laid out the road that the
race would follow. He knew all the bumps and bends along the
way, saw when the path would be smooth and level and when it
would veer off to a steep incline. He knew the green, blooming
meadows the road would journey through, and the hot desert tracks
that would seem to extend as far as the eye could see. The One who
went ahead and marked the race knew every opponent that would
be encountered along the way. He went ahead and planned places
of rest and refreshment, and He laid out stretches that would push
and challenge the runners beyond what they would feel capable of
achieving. He mapped it all out, marking the race He personally
designed for each runner.

This life is not a collection of coincidental circumstances. It is
not a journey of happenstance and luck (or lack thereof). The race
we are each running was specifically marked by God. He went ahead
of us and designed a path that would bring us the best we could
possibly receive. The road does not always appear good to us, and at
times, we feel like we have run out of steam, but we need to throw off
everything that hinders and entangles us and fix our eyes on Jesus,

the author and perfecter of our faith. He not only marked out the race before us, but He is also running it right alongside us. We are not in this alone. He is our strength and endurance, and He will see us through to the finish line.

CHAPTER 4

DIFFICULT TIMES

Even in the Storms

Do not fear, for I have redeemed you; I have
summoned you by name; you are mine.
When you pass through the waters, I will be with you;
and when you pass through the rivers,
they will not sweep over you.
When you walk through the fire, you will not be burned;
the flames will not set you ablaze.
For I am the LORD, your God, the Holy One of Israel, your Savior.
—Isaiah 43:1–3

If there is one thing that is certain in life, it is that we will unavoidably go through painful and difficult times. We will face circumstances that are scary, uncertain and at times may even be downright dangerous. Our paths will lead us to moments when we are caught in the surging waters of fear and the unknown. We will find ourselves in the fires of adversity, rejected or being hard pressed on every side. God's word makes it very clear that those moments are not simply a possibility, they are a certainty. It does not say "if" you find yourself in the storms and fires of life, it says, "when." So what of those times? What hope is there for us when we are in the thick of our darkest days?

Isaiah 43 begins with the most precious and vital truth we need to keep at the forefront of our minds. We have no cause for fear, because God has redeemed us, He has beckoned each one of us by name and we are forever His, never to fall from His arms. Dwell on that for a moment. God rescued you from the clutches of sin and death. While you were wrapped in chains of eternal separation from Him, He paid your debt and redeemed your life. He called you by name, stirring your heart and mind to hear His call to life and salvation. The moment you turned to Him and accepted His saving grace, all that separated you from Him fell away and you became His daughter, His son. You became His. That is the foundation of a hope and security that cannot be taken from us, no matter where we go and what we face.

And so our lives carry on, and at times we find ourselves in the midst of a raging sea, and it seems as though we will drown under the weight of that which comes against us. We feel engulfed and surrounded by doubts and fears that seem to seep into every nook and cranny. At other times, we are caught in a fiery furnace of opposition and pressure, flames that appear as though they will consume and destroy all that we hold dear. But hold fast! In the raging sea, in the blazing flames, look beside you. You are not alone! Your God, the very One who already rescued you from eternal death, who calls you His child, is beside you in it. His hand stays the waves and stops them from crashing over you. His protection surrounds you in the fire and does not allow it to consume you.

When you find yourself in circumstances that are scary and uncertain and threaten to be your destruction, remember that God is with you. He will prevent them from destroying you. As certain as the difficult times of life are, so too is the certainty of His protection and faithfulness. Trust your Redeemer. He loved you enough to rescue you when you were still His enemy. How much more will He undoubtedly rescue you from the fiercest battles you face now that you are His child. He will not prevent you from ever going through the battles, but He *will* remain faithfully by your side in the midst of them, and He alone will guard your life. He is the Lord, your faithful God, your Savior. Nothing can separate you from His love.

Set Your Face Like Flint

Because the Sovereign LORD helps me, I will not be disgraced.
Therefore have I set my face like flint,
and I know I will not be put to shame.
–Isaiah 50:7

Fight the good fight of faith.
—I Timothy 6:12

As you walk with God, your faith will be challenged. At every turn and in every decision, you will be confronted by voices that will try to shake your confidence in God and your obedience to Him. You will be tempted to doubt, to fear, to question if following God and trusting Him is all in vain. You will face situations that seem to contradict God's promises, and at times it will seem you are alone in the battle. Typically when we are confronted with those times, we want to flee. We want to cover our ears and shut our eyes and block out everything that challenges our faith.

In I Timothy, Paul admonishes Timothy to "fight the good fight of faith." A fight involves an opponent, and in every fight that opponent is going to do everything he can to win. We face an opponent on this walk of faith, and he fights dirty. He is the father of lies, and every word that comes out of his mouth is designed to steal, kill, and destroy. He does not care when you are feeling weak. He does not care when you are having a bad day. He does not care when you do not want to fight. He will come at you every chance he gets, and he aims for where it hurts most.

However, his blows do not have to hit the mark. You can fight back. Every time you are challenged to doubt God, to question His character, to let go of your hope in His promises, turn to Him. Turn to His word. Investigate who He is and how He has responded to

His people since the beginning of time. Allow the weapons that are intended to destroy you to be used as tools that refine and sharpen you. Take the whispers of foolishness and naivety and hopelessness, and hold them up against what God says.

As you do so, you will gradually grow more and more confident in who your God is and what He promises, until you find your face set as flint, unflinchingly resolved to maintain your gaze on God. You will grow ever more confident that as long as you are living your life for God, He will never let you be disgraced. With every accusation Satan throws in your face, every doubt he whispers in your ear, every temptation he lures you to chase after, pick up your sword, God's word, and fight back. Stand firm in who God is and who you are in Him. Plant your feet firmly on the path God has you on and let nothing move you. You cannot choose whether or not to be in the fight, but you can choose how you respond. Allow God to use every blow Satan throws at you to train and strengthen you.

You can never out-trust God. You cannot place more faith in Him than He is able to live up to. Continue on, allowing every challenge and opposition to develop a faith that cannot be shaken. Fight the good fight of faith, knowing that with God on your side, nothing can stand against you.

The Deadly Seed of Doubt

And the LORD God commanded the man, "You are free
to eat from any tree in the garden; but you must not
eat from the tree of the knowledge of good and evil, for
when you eat from it you will certainly die." ...
Now the serpent was more crafty than any of the wild animals
the LORD God had made. He said to the woman, "Did God
really say, 'You must not eat from any tree in the garden'?"
The woman said to the serpent, "We may eat fruit from
the trees in the garden, but God did say, 'You must
not eat fruit from the tree that is in the middle of the
garden, and you must not touch it, or you will die.'"
"You will not certainly die," the serpent said to the woman.
"For God knows that when you eat from it your eyes will be
opened, and you will be like God, knowing good and evil."
—Genesis 2:16–17, 3:1–5

Trust and doubt—two of the most powerful elements of any
relationship—one produces unity and provides security and
steadfastness even in times of trial and difficulty. The other produces
division and fear and corrodes security even in the best of times.
One allows for freedom and vulnerability with the recipient of trust
while the other erects walls of suspicion and self-defense toward the
recipient of doubt. For any relationship to thrive and be healthy, there
must be trust.

Is it any wonder, then, that the root of every attack Satan throws
at us in our relationship with God is doubt in who God is? Consider
the very first time interaction between humans and Satan. At the
core of his questions to Eve lies a seed of doubt that Satan plants in
her mind. His questions send out roots of suspicion about God and
the reasons behind His instructions, tendrils that wrap themselves

around Eve's mind and lead her to question if God is in fact holding out on her. Maybe God is not truly protecting her from death but is instead trying to keep her from something good, something she ought to have, deserves to have. Maybe His interest is not really to keep her healthy and free but is instead to limit and short-change her. Satan twists God's words and leads Eve to believe that God cannot be trusted and that her best interest lies in the very thing God is protecting her from, and the result, just as God said, is death.

Satan is not creative, and in truth he does not have to be. His tactic used against the first two people on earth is still as successful now as it was then. At every opportunity, Satan whispers in our minds doubt about God, His word and His character. The doubts boil down to one question: is God lying? Whether the question relates to His provision, His love, His forgiveness, or His protection and guidance in our lives, every doubt comes down to the question, is God telling the truth? Can He truly be trusted?

Satan knows if he can send even just one root of doubt into the heart of our relationship with God, fear and suspicion will break up the foundation of our trust and leave us vulnerable and exposed to even more of Satan's lies. If he can get us to question who God is, everything else will quickly crumble—our faith, our worship, our surrender. Rather than living in the security and freedom of God's love and, in response, desiring to serve God with our lives, we will become wrapped in chains of fear and hopelessness, and be driven into isolation through self-preservation and believing the only one we can count on in life is ourselves.

You are not a helpless victim in the attack. You are not defenseless against the whispers of doubt. When they come, and they surely will, you have a place to run. Turn to God's word. Dig into it and see how many times the Bible testifies of His trustworthiness, how repeatedly He assures you there is no reason to fear. Stand on the truth, the unshakeable, absolute truth of the word of God. Regain your footing, steady your feet, and the next time Satan suggests to you that God cannot be trusted, refute his lies. Do not shrink back. Do not allow the seed to take root in your mind. Stand firm in the truth of God's word and declare your trust in who He is. Your God cannot lie. Your God does not disappoint. Your God has a future planned for you and is working all things together for your good. Guard your mind and fall once again into the trustworthy arms of your Savior and King.

Be on Guard

Be alert and of sober mind. Your enemy the devil prowls
around like a roaring lion looking for someone to devour. Resist
him, standing firm in the faith, because you know that the
family of believers throughout the world is undergoing
the same kind of sufferings.
—I Peter 5:8–9

Finally, brothers and sisters, whatever is true, whatever
is noble, whatever is right, whatever is pure, whatever is
lovely, whatever is admirable – if anything is excellent
or praiseworthy – think about such things.
—Philippians 4:8

We demolish arguments and every pretension that
sets itself up against the knowledge of God, and
we take captive every thought to make it obedient to Christ.
—2 Corinthians 10:5

Every single day, we are in a battle. Believers and unbelievers alike
face an enemy who is out to kill, steal, and destroy. If you have
claimed Christ as your Savior, you are His forever, and Satan can no
longer have you, but that does not mean he stops the attack. Even
if he cannot have your soul, he will do everything he can to render
you ineffective and broken. There are general, all-encompassing ways
that Satan aims his attack at all believers, but there are also strategic,
personal ways he comes at each one of us, targeting our weaknesses
and struggles. One of his biggest fields of attack is in the mind. If he
can distract you from God's truth, from who you are in Christ, and
from God's perfect plan and purpose for your life, and replace those

things with fear, doubt, anxiety, insecurity, and impatience, he has you right where he wants you.

Philippians 4:8 provides a measuring rod for identifying thoughts that are from God and based on His word, and thoughts that are lies and attack from Satan. Follow the instruction of 2 Corinthians 10:5 and take every thought captive. Hold it up against God's word and examine if it is true, noble, right, pure, lovely and admirable. If so, it is from God. If it is not, reject the thought and demolish the argument formed against your mind by the enemy.

Be on guard, put on the armor of God (Ephesians 6), and stand firm in the faith. Remember that you are not fighting in your own strength or ability; you have the God of all creation on your side and He will never let the righteous fall.

Affliction

Before I was afflicted I went astray,
but now I obey your word ...
It was good for me to be afflicted
so that I might learn your decrees ...
I know, LORD, that your laws are righteous,
and that in faithfulness you have afflicted me ...
If your law had not been my delight,
I would have perished in my affliction.
I will never forget your precepts,
for by them you have preserved my life.
Save me, for I am yours; I have sought out your precepts.
—Psalm 119:67, 71, 75, 92–94

We typically think of affliction as always being an attack from
Satan or part of what we are subject to because of this life in which
we live. However, these passages make it very clear that sometimes
the affliction comes directly from God's hand for several potential
purposes:

- to call us back (v. 67),
- to teach us His ways and laws (v. 71),
- to demonstrate His faithfulness (v. 75), or
- to test our hearts and reveal whether or not we truly desire
  Him and His ways (v. 92–94)

If God did not love us, He would leave us alone. But He does love
us, and with love comes discipline.

God Is in the Dire

It was not you who sent me here, but God.

—Genesis 45:8

Joseph was the favorite of his father's sons, but he was despised by his brothers. He was stripped of his prized cloak, thrown into a cistern, and sold by his brothers to foreigners for twenty pieces of silver. He was taken to Egypt to be a slave, falsely accused, and thrown into prison where he was forgotten about for two years. He endured the loss of his entire family and everything he had ever known, and he spent years in a prison cell for a crime he did not commit. Betrayal, isolation, rejection, confusion, hopelessness, fear, sadness, anger—those are just a few things Joseph had to have been feeling through all of it, and rightfully so. He was mistreated, devalued and thrown into scary, dire circumstances that he did not cause and that he had no control over.

And yet, after enduring those years of grief and despair, he came through it declaring that God, not his brothers, was the one who had brought him to Egypt. He declared that God's hand was behind everything that had led up to that place and time, during which God used Joseph to save countless lives from dying of starvation during a seven-year famine. He did not begrudge his brothers for what they had done, he held no bitterness or resentment, and he did not even accuse them of ruining his life. He recognized that God had orchestrated it all for a much larger purpose than any of them could have imagined.

Do we respond as Joseph did? When we endure pain and crushing circumstances that we have no control over, it is really hard to see how any of it, let alone all of it, could be used for our good. When we face rejection and betrayal and lose all that we hold dear, we cannot imagine how any of it could be in our best interest. But the unrelenting hope that we have, even when we do not *feel* hopeful, is that God is using it all for a much grander purpose than we know. The pain is real, and He knows that. The struggle is intense, and He knows that too. But He also knows that if we will just endure a little longer, if we will turn to Him and entrust ourselves into His hands even as our hearts are breaking, He will use every single moment for our good. He will bring out of it a blessing and greater purpose than we ever could have experienced without it. He is right there beside you in it, catching every single tear that falls from your eye, carrying you through to glory.

Temptations

Since the children have flesh and blood, he too shared in their humanity so that by his death he might break the power of him who holds the power of death - that is, the devil - and free those who all their lives were held in slavery by their fear of death. For surely it is not angels he helps, but Abraham's descendants. For this reason he had to be made like them, fully human in every way, in order that he might become a merciful and faithful high priest in service to God, and that he might make atonement for the sins of the people. Because he himself suffered when he was tempted, he is able to help those who are being tempted.

—Hebrews 2:14–18

The concept that Jesus suffered when He was tempted had never struck me before until recently. It is astounding to discover that because Jesus was fully human (while remaining fully God), facing temptation was not any easier for Him than it is for us. It speaks of misgiving we often have about struggling. We tend to think if we are not strong all the time or if we struggle with temptations, then we must be weak or lack enough faith. However, Jesus proves this thinking wrong by His own experience. Suffering and struggling when faced with trials and temptations is not wrong or a sign of weakness; it is a part of being human. What is important is how we respond to the temptation—if we resist it or if we succumb to it. It is in Christ's responses in His own life that we see His perfection. Though He was tempted, He never sinned; He never gave in to it.

Thank God that He does not expect us to never struggle or suffer in the challenges we face. Thank God that He provided us with a faithful High Priest who intercedes on our behalf and gives us strength in the struggles. Thank God that He does not look down upon or condemn our struggles but that through experiencing them Himself, He understands them. He is the Father of mercy and compassion.

The Enemy of Your Soul

Be alert and of sober mind. Your enemy the devil prowls
around like a roaring lion looking for someone to devour.
Resist him, standing firm in the faith, because you know that
the family of believers throughout the world is undergoing
the same kind of sufferings.
—I Peter 5:8–9

Be on your guard; stand firm in the faith; be courageous;
be strong.
—I Corinthians 16:13

Submit yourselves, then, to God. Resist the
devil, and he will flee from you.
—James 4:7

You have an enemy, an enemy who is hell-bent on maiming you,
crippling you, destroying you, and in the long run, killing you. He
fights dirty, using manipulation, lies, deception, temptation, and
full-on attacks. At times he makes no attempts to hide his hatred
toward you, but more often than not, he disguises himself as your
friend, as the one looking out for your best interest, as someone
who is on your side, trying to loosen you from stifling rules and
obligations. He appears as an angel of light, someone who truly
gets you and seemingly offers you every desire of your heart, every
satisfaction that you hunger.

But under his disguise is someone who wants to inflict as much
pain and misery in your life as possible. He whispers words of honey
into your ear, tempting you to swallow what appears to be sweet and
satisfying, knowing that even just one drop is enough to poison you.
He tempts you to believe that your heart and emotions should be your

compass in life. Whatever feels right to you, whatever and whoever makes you feel happy at any given moment, that is what you should pursue, that, in fact, to deny yourself of those things is unhealthy, unnatural.

He whispers to you that moral obligation and living by God's standards is antiquated and bigoted, and it will leave you unhappy, unsatisfied, and missing out in life. He paints in your mind pictures of "what could be" if you would just follow him and stray from the straight and narrow. He tells you that you deserve what makes you happy and you deserve to have your cake and eat it too, and that anyone who tells you differently is your real enemy.

He warps God's character and distorts the truth of who God is, deceiving you to believe that God is out to get you, that God is keeping things from you and holding out on you. He whispers that living by God's standards and trusting Him is foolish and will lead to certain disappointment. He tells you that God does not really love you; He does not really care about your life. Satan holds fruit out to you that appears to be so full of nectar and promise, all the while laughing to himself at how easily we are deceived and how willing we are to swallow poison.

It is time to wake up to your enemy. It is time to recognize his true character, his true purpose. His only goal is to kill, steal, and destroy, and he will do so through any means possible. He wants to destroy your heart, mind, marriage, family, job, and reputation. He wants to wrap chains around you so tightly that you are drowning in a sea of guilt, anxiety, fear, and hopelessness. He promises you the world, but he can only deliver death. If you are saved by the redeeming blood of Jesus Christ, he cannot have your soul, but do not think that means you are exempt from his attacks. He hates your God, and he wants nothing more to destroy the thing that God loves most—you.

Brother, sister, stand guard. Do not be deceived by Satan's lies. Do not listen to his whispers and false promises. Recognize that he is the enemy of your soul and stand firm in the name of Jesus Christ. Anything that comes at you that contradicts God's word and character, anything that presents itself as alluring or in your best interest but does not match what God says to be true, pure and right, reject and push away. See beyond the disguise and refuse to grant your enemy victory in the battle. You are in a fight for your life, and the worst thing you can do is deny the reality of it. Be on guard against the devil, who prowls around like a lion, searching for someone to devour. Allow yourself to stray away from God, and the devil will laugh as he wraps each link of chain around you. Draw close to God, resisting the devil, and he will flee.

The Battle Belongs to the Lord

We do not know what to do, but our eyes are on you.
—2 Chronicles 20:12

Do not be afraid or discouraged because of this vast army.
For the battle is not yours, but God's.
—2 Chronicles 20:15

In 2 Chronicles 20, Judah is being attacked by the Moabites, Ammonites, and Meunites. All the people of Judah come together to seek the Lord's help, and King Jehoshaphat cries out to Him. The king declares who God is, that He rules over all kingdoms, and that all power is in His hands. He acknowledges that it was by God's deliverance that the Israelites came to live in that land and not by the people's own strength or power. Now in the face of the approaching enemy, Jehoshaphat cries out to God, recognizing that the enemy army is too strong for them to defeat on their own. He and all the people are trembling, aware of their helplessness and need for a rescuer. Nestled in his prayer is a beautifully simple, vulnerable plea: "We do not know what to do, but our eyes are on you."

Have you ever been there? That is a silly question; we all have been at one time or another. Maybe you are there right now. An approaching army floods your line of vision and leaves you trembling. The attack seems imminent and appears to result in certain defeat. You know the limits of your own strength and that the battle exceeds those limits. In those moments of trepidation, we can respond in one of two ways. We can allow ourselves to become so overridden with fear that we freeze and allow ourselves to be crushed. We can choose to accept defeat and lie down where we are, allowing the attack to come and destroy our hope and faith without even attempting to fight. Or we can be as the people of Judah were. We can cry out to God. We can acknowledge that though we do not have the strength to withstand the enemy ourselves, He does. In the face of our uncertainty and fear, we can choose to look up and focus our eyes on our rescuer, believing Him able and willing to save.

God's response to the people is so beautiful. He meets them right where they are, in the midst of their trembling, and soothes them with words of comfort and protection. He tells them not to be afraid, not to be discouraged, and not to take it upon themselves to feel responsible for defeating the enemy. He assures them that the battle is not theirs to fight, it is God's—God, who is all powerful, who rules over all kingdoms and nations, who holds everything in the palm of His hands. He whispers those same words of comfort to you now. He soothes you with reassurance of His presence, love, and protection. He reminds you that this battle is not yours to fight, the enemy is not yours to defeat. It is God's. He is the One who fights for you. He is the One who crushes your enemies.

Today, in whatever you are facing, do not freeze in the face of adversity and allow hopelessness or fear to consume you. Do not assume the responsibility of trying to defeat your enemies in your own strength and ability. Cry out to God. Acknowledge His sovereignty. Remind yourself of His deliverance in the past. Call upon Him now on this battlefield and resolve that, though you do not know what to do, your eyes are on Him. He waits with anticipation for your ask. He longs to answer you with those same comforting, redeeming words. No matter what you are facing, train your eyes on God, for this battle is not yours but His, and He is faithful to save!

If My People

If my people, who are called by my name, will humble
themselves and pray and seek my face and turn from
their wicked ways, then I will hear from heaven,
and I will forgive their sin and will heal their land.
—2 Chronicles 7:14

There is no shortage of issues and difficulties that we face in this
country and across the world. When we come before the Lord, heavy-
hearted from the moral state of all we see around us, we would do
well to consider a few questions as we begin to pray, questions such
as, what is on the heart of God for this land? What would He have
us ask for?

We need to look no further than 2 Chronicles 7:14 to find His
response. Every person who claims salvation through Jesus Christ is
considered one called by His name. As such, we, Christians, bear the
responsibility of following God's instruction in this passage in order
to see healing in our land. We have fallen into the same sin that led
to Lucifer's fall: pride. Through self-reliance, self-focus, and self-
indulgence, we have put ourselves in the place of God in our lives. We
have made idols of ourselves, our happiness, and our satisfaction, and
turned away from God. It is a harsh reality that stares us in the face
when we look at the state of our land and culture. So what are we to
do? Is all lost without hope of restoration? Thank God, by His grace
and mercy, never. He makes it so plain through four progressive steps
which lead to deliverance and healing.

First, we need to humble ourselves. We need to fall on our knees
before God and confess our pride and self-reliance rather than God-
reliance. We need to recognize who God is, and who we are (and are
not), and declare Him holy and on the throne.

We need to pray. In I Chronicles 5:18–22, when the Reubenites, the Gadites and the half-tribe of Manasseh were in battle against their enemies, they won the war because they cried out to God and trusted in Him. They recognized that God was their only hope for victory and relied on Him for their deliverance. We need to do the same here and now. We are surrounded by enemies, visible and invisible, who are out to steal, kill and destroy. We need to cry out to God in the battle now as they did then, trusting Him to answer. He will not disappoint.

We need to seek His face. *Seek* means "to go in search of; to try to discover something or someone." We need to search to understand God's mind, His heart, and His will. We need to pursue Him as one pursues hidden treasure.

Lastly, we need to turn from our wicked ways. The first three steps are in vain if we do not turn from our ways of disobedience and repent of the things that separate us from God. To continue in those things would negate any humbling of ourselves, any praying, and any seeking His face, because it would demonstrate that we still want to live our lives our own way rather than God's way. We need to surrender all we have to Him, placing Him first above it all, and choose, moment by moment, to live lives of righteousness in honor to Him.

His promise in response to these four steps is amazing; He will hear us, He will forgive our sin, and He will heal our land. It does not matter how long we prevailed in our wrong-living. It does not matter how far we strayed from Him or how long we have put ourselves in His rightful place. If we will come before Him in true humility, seeking to know Him and live for Him, He will hear, forgive, and restore. And God does not lie; His word is His promise.

Now more than ever before, the children of God need to rise up and restore Him to His rightful place. We need to stop looking to the government for the answers—it does not have them. We need to stop trying to figure out which political candidate will be best able to save and restore our country—they will all fail. Our help is not found in men (or women); it is found in God alone. May He ignite a fire across His church, a spark that burns as a revival of His people, which beckons all hearts to turn to Him and be saved. May we rise up and stand firm on His gospel of salvation through Jesus Christ, declaring hope and life to a dying world. Rising up begins on our knees.

Printed in the United States
By Bookmasters